PAUSING

For David, RJ, Ashley, Marion and Eden

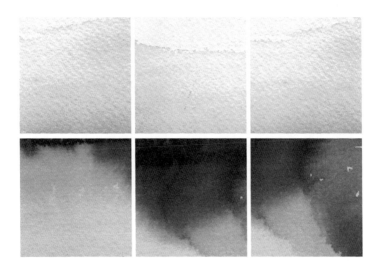

PAUSING

Reflections in Poems and Art by

MARIETTA PATRICIA LEIS

POEM INDEX

INTRODUCTION

In the cold and rainy month of March 2011 I was an Artist in Residence at the Morris Graves Foundation, The Lake, in Northern California. The late Graves was an artist whom I admired for his life and work—they were not separate—I felt privileged to stay in his studio. His environments are fabled stories and The Lake did not disappoint; an inspired place of lake, redwood trees, and a home and studio of Japanese influence.

It is a place of grace, peace and beauty that encouraged me to press my life's pause button. Living and working in this setting inspired me to think in verse. These poems reflect my state of being or my observations as I passed through my days painting there in tranquility. The simple passing of my days resulted in this work. I hope you sense this simplicity in this volume.

- M P L

*Only in quiet waters do things
mirror themselves undistorted.*

–Hans Margolius

PAUSING

AWAKENED

I can feel the calm of the morning
after a night of nature's roar

The sun is shining across the treetops
with blue sky peeping through

I can't wait to dress and go outside
to walk among newly bathed friends

What joy in dewdrops and soaked earth
when I can be a companion instead of hiding
within

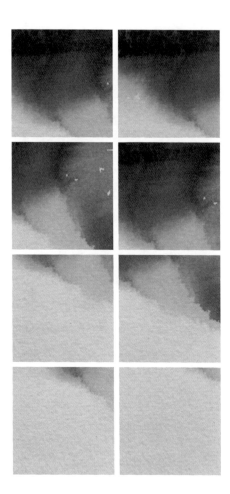

PATIENCE

This place evolved with
time and labor
No small task to clear
pesky intruders
and uncover the armature
of beauty

It took seeing
and imagining
and planning
and physical endurance
to carve out
The Lake from its wilderness

Needed was the
discipline of knowing
what to keep
and what would be gained
from discarding

Decisions made with restraint
and vision
and love

DARK LAKE

A lake so dark
sap green,
sometimes black

Mysterious
not foreboding
—calm

Surrounded by
green life, and
reflecting it back
with deeper, thoughtful
understanding

FOG

The fog rolls in
over the Lake
shrouding my eyes

Reflections echoing truth
in their subtle
refrain

Ducks alighting
in the lake
with grace

I weep

FREE

No locks, keys or bolts
I can go in and out
without the burden
So novel, so free
Lucky me!

RAIN

You do wonder
how it can rain so much
Where does all the water go?
Does it soak through to
the other side of the globe
and irrigate the rice paddies
of China?
Maybe then its worth
the endless puddles and mud here

THE HOST

I follow the path
turn the doorknob
hold my breath
and enter his space

There is a soft humming
vibration from the walls
the furnishings, the books
—all

His chair is by the window
where he read
looking out at his
Lake

Listening deeply from
my heart with my eyes
softly gazing
I still

I'm touched by the beauty
of his silence and gratefully
accept what he cares
to reveal

FRIEND

Ah, Blue Heron
how gracious
that you kept
me company tonight

Your pose and poise
reflected in the lake
and
in my heart

JAPAN'S HAVOC
(Earthquake and Tsunami, March, 2011)[1]

Thunder rattles my sleep
Lightning illuminates the dark room
I acknowledge God's roar
And slip back into oblivion

How safe I feel in this nest
Warmed by the wood stove
Protected by 800 year old trees
And beauty abounding everywhere

Here the Japanese landscapes soothe
With contemplative artistry
While across the sea, ravaged by nature
Japan is undone

I pay homage for the inspiration
That created this place of calm
I say prayers for those who now suffer
And those who no longer do

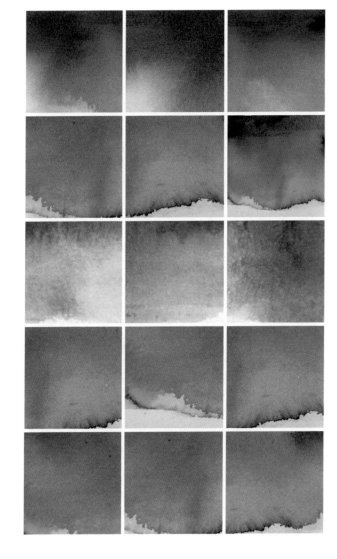

MARCH

Aha, the sun breaks through
this fickled March
between the wind, rain and hail
Just a tease of things to come
and make me both excited
to play outdoors again
and sad to leave my cozy
comfort-zone nest

TRAILS

The trails are marked
so I won't get lost
The rain has softened
the earth and I slip

Not too bad but enough
to tread carefully
as I view the wonder
with each step

Careful to look up
not always at my feet
Up at the trees
the majestic elders

Also to look out at the
vistas of ocean and land
Close up are budding
flowers and shrubs

Walking records this
journey of beauty
Each step memorizing
the feelings evoked

DUCKY

A little brown duck
swims in a little brown lake
gliding with no effort
in the now stilled waters

Taking a reprieve before
the wind and rain
come again to disturb
the now smooth surface

The level of the lake
is higher now
and the duck
is lifted to new views

No wonder he moves slowly
to take it all in
feeling big and worldly
in his little lake

FOGGY

The fog mimics
how I sometimes
perceive poorly

Not clearly
denying truth
hiding

It is possible to see
through the
murkiness

Deciding clarity
is worth
the risk of knowing

But growing up
is not
easy

INTERRUPTIONS

On the placid lake
a small lone duck
leaves a long trail

A single fish
breaks the water
the circle resonates to shore

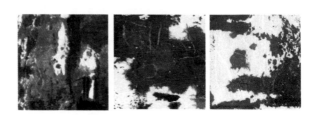

AGAIN

You're back old friend
to share another evening

I'm surprised and glad
to have your company again

Once was grand
I savor twice with gratitude

Your focus is a model
Your calm an inspiration

GOOD NIGHT

The Lake settles down
calmly in evening
after a tumultuous day
of churning and rocking

Peacefully now the
reflected trees mirror
green and mysterious
in the last light

Ducks glide softly
for their day's final
meal and fish jump
before sleeping

Heaven is glimpsed from
my studio window
tucking in for the night
resting for tomorrow

MOODS

Gloom takes hold
with cold and darkness
at daybreak

Suddenly light breaks
through and in a
moment life changes

BLUE

Blue, I see blue
slithering into
the gray sky

Ah, that means
work instead of
another dreamy day

TABLEAU

Everything here is framed
My senses stir with each glance
I see a Japanese landscape
And then a still life of glass bottles

So many things to quiet me
No detail can be hurried by
Not the cattails, nor the water lilies
Not the Grandfather trees

Each rock is placed perfectly
Thoughtfully but never contrived
With an artist's vision
And a man's soul

It's a gift to behold beauty
at every turn
Never failing to delight
and surprise

MERCIFULLY COMPLICATED

We're none of us easy to know
That would be too simple

It wouldn't be any fun
The excavation is the thrill

Finding out a little bit
About you
About me

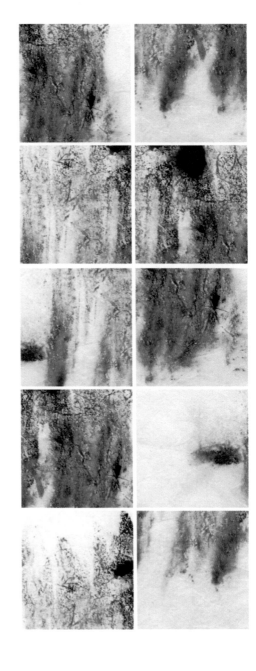

TREE

Oh majestic tree
how safe I feel
hugging your stable trunk

Although you tower over me
you protect my soul
from unbelieving

MEDITATING

No need for a formal practice to sit here
Each glance bids me to breathe slowly
Each breath centers me in gratitude
Here

Now

MORNING

The morning has awakened
in peace
The calm is tangible

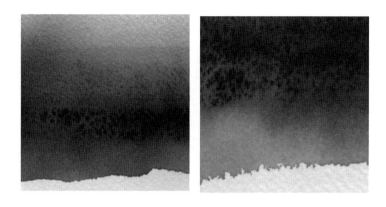

THE LAKE

Serenity describes
The Lake best
As though the world
is at peace and rest

HAIL

Hail to the hail
pelting in fury
and gusty anger to
break the monotony
of a gray silence

It is a good show
none-the-less
surprising
with its energy
and vigor

The ions must be
rearranged now
for a sleepy day
has turned lively
and expectant

SORTING IT OUT

Editing
Selecting
Focus

A way of cultivating
the mind and heart

Reducing
Restraint
Clarity

A way of making room for
peace and calm

SHIFT

Dark and dreary
the day seems

Then a sliver of light
and it all shifts

THE ROWBOAT

The little rowboat
just right for one
sits in its boat house
tempting, taunting

Oar ready
vest ready
boater not ready
yet

GREEN

Luxurious and luscious
cool and nurturing
many nuances
many shades

Life and growth
abound
beckoning
bewitching

This verdant paradiso
is all ripe and ready
to spring forth
to love

A SECRET PLACE

Tucked away from all
the noise and fright

A bowl of water and a
stand of trees

Hidden from today's
life roar

Secretive, quiet
holding its breath

Not to be found out
and spoiled

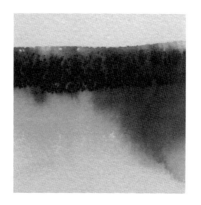

TIME

Time is a peculiar thing
We speak of it as
a powerful adversary
that controls our pitiful lives

Time defeats our defenseless selves
in almost every battle
It dictates the terms of
our lives and possibilities

Time avoids our anguished
pleas for more time for our
chores, exercise, catching up
and for sleep, yes sleep

But this recent experiment
of no phones, no emails,
no computers, no newspapers
brought the truth to light

Time can be abundant and
my best friend
if good choices prevail

I am in chase of me—not thee

SUNSHINE

The sun finally
shows its laughing face
on the day before I leave

I thought it had forgotten
its duties, this address
or maybe waited to surprise

It wasn't missed as
much as expected
but I'm warmed that it's here

ADIEU

My visit with you is over
I'm leaving sated—filled
Knowing you a little better
But knowing myself more

FOOTNOTE

[1] Leis is involved with several international arts organizations that bring attention through exhibitions to the ongoing tragedies of the Fukushima nuclear disaster.

THANK YOU

My thanks to the Morris Graves Foundation and to Director, Robert Yarber, assistant to the late Morris Graves. Also to Desiree Yarber. Their efforts have kept the spirit of Graves alive. Their kindness and facilitation enhanced my experience.

-MPL

MARIETTA PATRICIA LEIS

Marietta Patricia Leis is a visual artist who lives and works in New Mexico. Her work encompasses multiple media including paintings, drawings, sculpture, installation and yes, poetry. There is always an element of the sensory in Leis' art—a texture, a color, a deep space—something to engage the senses of the viewer. Her abstract, reductive color fields run the risk of invisibility, but silence, patience, and deep listening gratify the viewer. Leis' frequent travels and artist residencies inspire her work.

www.mariettaleis.com